N⊕W IS
ETERNITY

⊕

Comfort and Wisdom for Difficult Hours
from Christoph Friedrich Blumhardt
and Johann Christoph Blumhardt

THE PLOUGH PUBLISHING HOUSE

Text translated from *Jetzt ist Ewigkeit: Worte von Blumhardt Vater und Sohn*,
Ausgewählt von Dr. Alo Münch (Munich, Verlag Paul Müller, 1947);
Preface based on Alo Münch's introduction.

Cover Photograph: *Starry Night* by Vincent VanGogh / SuperStock

First English edition (hardcover): 1976
Revised translation (paperback): 1999

06 05 04 03 02 01 00   10 9 8 7 6 5 4 3 2

A catalog record for this book is available from the British Library

Library of Congress Cataloging-in-Publication Data

Blumhardt, Christoph, 1842-1919.
  [Jetzt ist Ewigkeit. English]
  Now is eternity : comfort and wisdom for difficult hours / from the
writings of Christoph F. and Johann C. Blumhardt.— Rev. translation.
    p. cm.
  Earlier English languge ed. (c1976) has authors' names reversed.
  ISBN 0-87486-993-5
  1. Meditations. I. Blumhardt, Johann Christoph, 1805-1880.
II. Title.

BV4834 .B51313 2000
242'.4—dc21
                                                    99-050833

Printed in the USA

In memoriam
WINIFRED M. HILDEL
1920–1999

⊕

RELATED PL⊕UGH TITLES

S⊕URCES

Texts on the these pages are by Christoph F. Blumhardt:
1, 2, 3, 5, 6, 7, 8, 9, 10, 11, 12, 14, 15, 16, 17, 18, 19, 21,
22, 23, 24, 26, 28, 29, 30, 31, 32, 33, 34, 36, 37, 39, 40,
41, 43, 44, 45, 46, 47, 49, 51, 53, 54, 56, 58, 60, 61, 63,
65, 66, 67, 68

Texts on the these pages are by Johann C. Blumhardt:
4, 13, 20, 25, 27, 35, 38, 42, 48, 50, 52, 55, 57, 59, 62, 64

Come home at last; come, end of loneliness...
to our thin dying souls against Eternity pressed.
STEPHEN SPENDER

⊕

PREFACE

T HE DEEPEST NEED each of us has, even if we are not conscious of it, is that of eternal life." With these words Christoph F. Blumhardt uncovers the root cause of so much that has gone wrong in modern life: the loss of any awareness of eternity. For most people nowadays, it is the temporal and transitory things of life that are most important. That is not surprising, for those things are immediate, tangible, and visible. But it is still lamentable, because it means that the eternal dimension of life – that part of it that is divine and thus enduring – falls by the wayside, unnoticed and unacknowledged.

When eternity is forgotten, human destiny is robbed of its real significance, and the goal of life limited to the search for fulfillment on an

earthly plane. Remembered, it enlarges our view
and, through what is best and noblest in us,
reminds us of the promise of another home on a
higher plane: the world from which we come,
and to which we must one day return.

To be mindful of eternity is to know that our
earthly existence will one day be overshadowed
by the eternal reality of everlasting life.

Anyone who opens our minds to this knowledge does us a great service. That is why the
words collected here, unassuming and simple
as they are, are so powerful, and so significant.
For Johann Christoph Blumhardt (1805–1880)
and his son, Christoph Friedrich Blumhardt
(1842–1919), "eternity" is not just another word
for the hereafter – for some vague, future haven
where the souls of the departed find rest. No.
For them eternity is a present reality whose
transformative power is already breaking into

⊕

×

time, and whose glory is already visible here and there, wherever there are eyes to see it. And so for us, it is a guide and a beacon, a source of strength, a fountain of hope that never fails. We need this hope urgently, no less than we need our daily bread.

The Editors
December 1999

IF WE are not active as part of a whole, working toward a higher goal, we will deteriorate inwardly and outwardly. Only if our hearts are in a task greater than ourselves will we thrive in earthly matters too. Society will deteriorate, physically and spiritually, unless each of its members has a task to fulfill for the sake of the common good, and for creation – for God.

WHETHER we are aware of it or not, eternity is our only joy. It strengthens us in our earthly life, which is ephemeral without eternity. Anything we might hope for in life, everything we have that brings us joy, is connected with the name of Jesus, the heavenly jewel sent us by the Father. And so, in the measure that we share in his name, the years of our life will be enfolded in heavenly things.

T O FEEL CLOSE to God is a great comfort. It is depressing to feel alone and forsaken, to think that we have been left to our own resources and must rely on our own strength. I would not want to live a single day without being able to feel that God's angels are around me, and around the whole world. I cannot live one day without believing that we are never alone.

It is wonderful to know what we live for, to know that what we do for our Lord is never wasted but will bear fruit in eternity. Yet we must not forget that whatever good we accomplish is not the result of our own strength. It happens only through the blood of Christ. If we forget this, all our efforts will fail, because we will lack the incentive to dispense with worthless things and seek the truth. Oh, how hard it is to draw oneself out of the vanity of one's own life!

PERHAPS the greatest danger that threatens us comes from being overly involved in the small, ordinary happenings of daily life – from becoming so enslaved by them that they fill our heart and soul. To go about life in this way is to go about unprotected, unaware, distracted, and removed from reality. Let us never allow ourselves to be dragged down by pettiness, or take the things of this earth so seriously that they burden us day after day. Let us live constantly in the Promise.

⊕

E MUST go down into the depths; that is our calling. Yet at the same time we must keep the heights in our hearts. Our human calling goes beyond death into eternity. Blessed are those who keep God's height in their own depths.

HEN WE have found the foundation that God gives us for our lives, we will be shown his light for all people, both in the visible and in the invisible world. And we will be given the certainty that our faith and our relationship with the Father, as well as our life on earth – fraught as it is with trials and darkness – can work for the good of the world and for humankind. That is our joy.

W E FIND ourselves in darkness, yet we
live in the light; we know sorrow, yet we
have joy; we are burdened, yet we have
wings to meet our God, the eternal light
and life of all creation. This is our joy now,
and in this joy we shall remain. We must
fight; we must hold the standard high; we
must let the light shine forth. We must
never be discouraged.

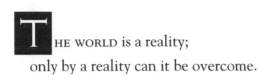

THE WORLD is a reality;
only by a reality can it be overcome.

JESUS MAKES all things new! That is our light. And with it we can look into the greatest depravities, into the darkest places of humanity, and still have confidence in the God who makes all things new in heaven and on earth. We are not called to establish new hells, but to declare war on sin and death in the strength of God, who is love.

UR THOUGHTS should not dwell too briefly on the Crucified One. We ought, rather, to surrender our entire being to him: "Very well, if I must die to myself, I must; but I shall do so in the name of the living God – under his judgment alone, and at the side of the Savior." If we can release the things that bind us in this manner, we will be saved, for a whole new life will begin for us. The old world must be given up in this way – at the cross, and through judgment – if the new world is to begin.

⊕

VERYTHING that exists on earth
has something mysterious hidden in it.
Every visible being carries the stamp
of the eternal.

EVEN THOUGH we have not yet reached true blessedness, we can hope for it, for we do have a Father in heaven. He is a loving Father, and we may call to him with hearts full of joy and confidence. In this certainty a wave of blessedness will come over us; and it will never leave us, even though we suffer deep anguish again and again. In this certainty we can weep and rejoice at the same time.

Die, and Jesus will live" means "Yield, give up your demands." Then, instead of Death, you will see Life. We must go through death not in order to die, but so we might rise again.

GAIN AND AGAIN we experience goodness – in tangible, material ways as well.
By this we see that though Jesus died,
he lives, and truly lives, among us.

As soon as we begin to live in God, our whole life will be transformed. Then we will marvel: so many things that used to burden us or tempt us to worry will suddenly seem quite insignificant.

R IGHT INTO DEATH we must go! That is our first lesson as disciples of Jesus: to live in the midst of death, so that the Risen One is glorified. Therefore we should not say, "In the midst of life we are surrounded by death," but "In the midst of death we are surrounded by life." We should not mourn, but praise. Words do not convey the import of this truth, but every heart must receive it: you need no longer struggle to escape the valley of death, or to run from it as from an overpowering enemy. Stand firm instead at the side of the Risen One, and proclaim life in the midst of death. Jesus conquered death, and through him, the source of power and light, life will be victorious even in the dead.

E, TOO, are promised resurrection. One could almost say that to die is to rise again. It was not meant that the Savior alone should rise from the dead. Why should it stop there? We do not just die when death comes to us; we die into a resurrection. We are meant to live. And thus our lives should bear the stamp of life – the stamp of resurrection.

IN GOD'S KINGDOM are gifts we cannot yet comprehend – wonderful gifts of life and immortality – and when we enter it, we will experience abundance at every step. But the kingdom is not just a future idea with no present reality. I hear from many a miserable person: "I have found happiness in my wretchedness, for the gift of the heavenly kingdom is already in my heart. In the midst of pain I can see God."

SATAN'S BONDS are not unbreakable: whoever tackles them in earnest, believing in Christ, the conqueror, can be freed. As He himself says, "The truth will set you free," and "If the Son sets you free, you will indeed be free." Indeed, the victory is already won, for our Lord sits at the right hand of God. He has received gifts that are his to give, even to those who deny him. And he will fight from above until all his enemies have been cast down as a footstool for his feet; until all creation – heaven and earth – can shout for joy. Who can comprehend the greatness of Jesus' victory? Yet we shall inherit it, as soon as we believe and accept his triumph, which is there for all to see.

As LONG as Jesus is my Lord,
I do not need anyone else; but I will
not be alone. For all heaven stands
with those who take a lonely stand
on earth for Jesus.

I S IT STILL POSSIBLE to spread the news of the true gospel? Is it still possible to see someone made new in Christ? So many people have given up, lost hope. But even if the whole world no longer believed in the possibility of transformation, we would still have to believe: Christ wants to create new people, here on this earth. People could die a blessed death before Christ came; comfort in life, and comfort in death, too, could be had before Christ. But he came to make new people, filled with the power of eternal life and radiant with the love of God, who is the light of truth and life.

CHRIST PROMISED US he would be with us: "I am with you to the end of the age." So in all our weakness and poverty he is here. He is present; he works signs and miracles, and in him we can rejoice.

ONCE WE really know Christ, we will enter a new world. Overwhelmed by the richness and diversity of the divine, we will take his power in our own lives for granted – power we had hardly believed possible. But that is what it means to have new life in Christ.

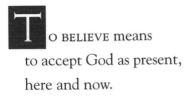

TO BELIEVE means
to accept God as present,
here and now.

To THINK only in terms of what is "natural," to expect help from the natural world alone – that is fanaticism! Yet to this day, if you forsake such help and depend on the Holy Spirit and the power of God, people will say you are deluded. In actual fact, however, there is no doubt that biblically speaking, it is unrealistic and deluded to depend on the world's sources of strength; and fanatical to rely on its nonsense as if it were the real help or remedy.

W ITH GOD nothing is impossible." He can make newborn people even of us; he is able to bring about total rebirth. He can transform godless people into godly ones, and children of Satan into children of God. Yes, with him nothing is impossible. And from him – through his omnipotence – each of us can expect the help we need. Through him we can find freedom from the bondage of much that would be otherwise impossible to escape or overcome.

WE ARE INDEPENDENT of time and season; a new year does not impress us. Our lives bear the mark of eternity, of the eternal God who created us in his image. He does not want us to be swallowed up in what is transitory, but calls us to what is eternal. And he shall make of us immortal, timeless beings filled with eternity.

THE TEMPTER has an easy time with people who lack insight into God's plans and his revelations, those without discernment. As for knowledge of what is true or untrue, let us not forget that in overthrowing the Tempter, Jesus placed the realities of heaven at our disposal. On our own we cannot rise above the laws of this world, but with Jesus we can. Believe it: the Savior is able to help us at *any* time and in *any* way. He can sustain us even without bread.

CHRIST must stand before you as the living one. Awake, my heart! Rejoice and be glad, and do not let darkness overcome you. Do not let the sadness of the times fill your mind; they are man's times. Live in God's time. Do not forget that Christ may draw near at any moment and guide you to heaven.

IN THE MIDST of temporal darkness we can be transplanted into everlasting light; in the midst of death we can have life and peace. So let us continue to work and trust that though there may still be shadows, they will soon be scattered. Those who hold firmly to Christ will enter God's kingdom, the kingdom without end. That is our comfort and hope.

EVERYWHERE people are being saved; that is, they are finding themselves in the new world where they can find fullness of joy even in the midst of all sorrow. To live in this new world – to live in the kingdom of God – that gives strength for life, strength for whatever must be suffered and borne; strength even in dying. It gives hope that whoever calls upon the name of the Lord shall be saved, and knowledge that divine powers are at work, even if silently, here and now.

I F WE HAVE the right attitude of faith to the Savior and to the promises the Father makes, a new light will dawn for us, and the cause of Christ will suddenly take on joy and radiance. We will have new hope: "Why, we had completely forgotten that there is a Holy Spirit, who can supersede the laws of everyday life!" And we will not mourn, neither over the unfortunate circumstances of our lives, nor over the state of the churches, nor even over the powers of sin and hell. Nor will we fear the dangerous days that are foretold, the days of the end times. If we have the light and power of the Holy Spirit, we shall not be confounded.

No MEDICINE can make you whole like faith in Jesus Christ, the physician of souls who gives health of body and soul for time and eternity. He gives all this to those who are willing to drink at his healing fountain.

HOW GREAT is God's protection over those who have faith! Indeed, the very angels stand ready to serve us. We do not see these hosts; but the time may come again when we are allowed to perceive their presence, as proof of God's plan of salvation, and a reminder of the truth in the stories of old. For in the end, according to his original intent, God will carry out a miracle greater than any he has performed thus far: the redemption of the whole world.

PEOPLE THINK that after they die everything will suddenly fall into place. But if you do not have eternal life here, do you really think it will be any better over there? What gives you that hope? It would seem to me that when people die they will be just the same afterward as before. If they see and hear nothing but themselves in this life, won't it be the same for them in the next? But if they are gripped by eternity while still on earth, then dying – the laying aside of the body – will pale in comparison to beginning a new life full of heavenly joys.

S SURELY AS the world sets its hopes on machines, I set my hopes on the power of the Spirit. It is so strong that it can reverse everything that seems doomed. The Spirit can bring about a new heaven, a new earth, and a new life – and we ourselves will see it.

NOT UNTIL we know something of the wonderful goodness of God – the great God of heaven and earth, whose kindness goes out to the lowliest and comes to their aid outwardly as well as inwardly – not until then will we know what God is and feel lifted and carried by his peace. As the Psalmist says, "We have a God who helps us, and a Lord who saves us from death." Oh, if only we had faith truly to comprehend how close God is to us!

THE MORE we draw on God's deeds in the past and treasure them, the more capable we will become of experiencing his history; that is, his continued working in the world today. Then we will see miracles – not magicians' tricks, but divine wonders. Let us be patient. The human vestment will still fall away, and then we will see what remains: deeds unlike anything recorded in the books of men.

E NEED powers from God so that we can attend to the things of this world in such a way that they gain value for eternity.

NCE WE ENTER into God's world –
the world of Jesus Christ – new potentials
open up. And as we become conscious of
them, in body or soul, we will be able to
ask for even more to be given.

GREAT THINGS happen when we believe in Christ: our thoughts and feelings are transformed, our behavior changes – our entire disposition is transformed. Happiness, thoughtfulness, love, and peace; inward calm and healing from defects of body and soul – all these things come with belief. It is like resurrection. But these gifts would surely be even more striking if we had greater faith and childlikeness – if we were more eager to attain the new nature.

So MANY people say, "What is life to me? I wish I were dead!" But those who talk like this have lost every trace of the Spirit; they have forgotten what a God-given treasure life is. To value life: that is the essential! Whenever a new person enters your house – your life – ask, "How can I make their life a joy?" Don't ask, "What is he worth?" or "What can she do for me?" Give love, and the rest will come of itself. But keep this question always in mind: "How can I bring joy to others?"

I T IS FUTILE to seek the essence of Christianity in words – even in the words of Jesus, for they can never be summed up, not by the best system. The essence of Christianity shows itself only as a gift from another world – though even then it is often obscured by great jumbles of "Christian" activity. Even so, each of us can hope for it, and find it for ourselves. Even the impossible can be made possible by the silent power that surrounds us and bubbles over with life and splendor.

WHEN MAN AND WOMAN still belonged
to God, that was Paradise; when they no
longer belonged to him, it came to an end.
Then Jesus, the Son of God, came into the
world, and it was Paradise again. It is really
that simple: those who came to Jesus and
were touched by him were filled with bliss;
they came to life inwardly and outwardly.
Jesus had words of life, and those around
him were as if in Paradise. It is the same
for us now: wherever there are words of
life, there is Paradise.

TODAY YOU will be with me in Paradise."
When Jesus is among us, these words hold
true, wherever we are.

CHRIST WANTS to appear to us today – hidden, perhaps, and perhaps only in Spirit – yet not without the clear beginnings of eternal life. Anyone who yields to this knowledge will recognize how real Christ is.

WHENEVER God's Word appears to us, the eternal spark within us emerges from the pit and rises toward the light. We become different people; our souls awake and become alive; our spirits are roused from sleep, and a longing for our origin – for God – arises in us. We become our true selves. When our eyes are opened to see Christ's splendor, we are totally transformed. And the opposite is true too: when our eyes do not receive his light, we remain utterly blind.

GOD sends powers of every kind to aid body and soul, and he bestows them as personal gifts. His powers surround us and accompany us in infinite ways; they are richly diverse.

G OD SHOWS US so much kindness! If we were to count all the good things he does for us even in one day, we would be amazed, yet we neither see nor perceive most of them. If only our awareness of God were such that it could swallow up the disagreeable things of the day! But it is usually the other way around: they tend to swallow up whatever is good and push it into the background. To attain a cheerful frame of mind would not be hard, if only we learned to accept God's love to us. Then we could ignore life's unpleasant circumstances, which – in light of his goodness – are as good as nonexistent.

WE LIVE in a time of death and dying – we must face that fact – and as time goes on our power must decrease. Yes, even the greatest physical strength – even the liveliest mind and heart – must grow weak. The law of dying surrounds everything we do and think and feel. But there is also a law of life that enters into this dying, and that is the Lord Jesus himself. He is the ever-living one; resurrected from the dead, he reaches out to us from the other world. He conveys the Spirit to us, and in the midst of our dying he refreshes and enlivens us with his grace, and with the promise of his coming.

WHEN ALL is said and done, the worst thing is to have faith and yet no faith: to believe and yet not really believe; to claim a Savior and yet not expect anything of him; to speak of a God before whom all knees must bend, and yet worry that the devil is mightier than he – and because of this to lack courage and confidence in asking for what we have been promised. How near our help would be, and how quickly it would come, if we truly relied on the Savior; if we were truly convinced that Jesus, our brother at God's right hand, has the power to save us, his children.

W E MUST VIE with those in heaven. Our task is to give light on earth, in earthly weakness; theirs is to give light in heaven, in eternal brightness. Who will do more? Let us be watchful, lest we are some day put to shame. It is the same race, though we are stationed at different posts, and the same goal. Let us press on together: they carrying out their duty above; we doing ours below.

GOD'S GOODNESS is more powerful than evil, though people claim the latter is stronger on earth. Good has the final power; it is invincible. That is the knowledge and hope in which we live.

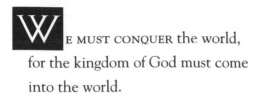

E MUST CONQUER the world, for the kingdom of God must come into the world.

PRAISE GOD – it is not impossible for those in heaven and those who strive toward it to be united, for we have a Savior in whom all become as one. In him those who have gone before and those who have stayed behind are brought together. It is not really a separation. Yes, in the Savior we are already one: we can have each other even today!

BELIEVE IT: heaven is open; it is no longer closed. We can imagine ourselves in heaven in God's glory, in the heart of our beloved Father – released from all sinister powers, and truly free. We may have every hope, for fulfillment is no longer far from us. And even though we may not yet ascend to heaven, we may still catch a glimpse of such an ascent. For just as our Lord rose ascended, so will we, since it is his will.

WERE GOD not a God who awakens the dead; were God a God who had to put up with human history as it is, were it impossible to wipe an old slate clean and begin again – then our faith in him would be purposeless. We might as well give it up today. But God is the creator of new life. And he is so great and strong that, though the world be headed toward destruction and death, he will yet steer it in the opposite direction, to life.

N THE CROSS our Lord fought through to complete victory: for him there is no grave anymore; no death. The most wicked enemy has been over-come. And so from now on, all – whether still alive, or already dead – belong to Him. He is the Lord of the dead as well as of the living.

WHEN SOMEONE who is close to me dies, I often wonder, "What is he doing now?" And then the answer comes: "Now he is going to school." For I would like to think that after Christ judges us, he takes us into his school, so that even in death we may learn to be God's children.

D YING is simply part of life; we must reckon with it as such. And haven't we seen how the Savior comes to many, even at the hour of death? How many there are whose eyes light up in the last moments, because he comes! Therefore be full of joy and hope, and remind yourself over and over that at death the Savior is coming again.

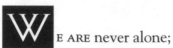

E ARE never alone;
if we have Jesus, his angels
are around us.

I F ONLY you had more faith; if only you could see that in spite of all your sorrows, the Lord is preparing great things for you! They may not be the things you expect, but they are surely much more wonderful. Whenever you suffer a loss – whenever a loved one departs from you or other sorrows come your way – trust and believe. And if your sorrows stay with you, pray. The Lord *is* working for you, and if you had any inkling of his love, your joy would break forth, even in your sadness.

W E CAN SAY with certainty that for those who die in the Lord, death has power over them only in this world, but no longer in the next. For them, death brings immortal life; for as the light of earthly life goes out, a new, heavenly light is kindled. Of Christ it was said, "In the body he was put to death; in the spirit he was brought to life." It is the same with those who die in the Lord.

OU MUST believe it: those who die
in the Savior are not lost! Do not mourn,
but live under the sign of the cross in the
spirit of Christ's victory. Once you entrust
your life to the Lord, death need no longer be a barrier: the curtain is pierced. To
be sure, you cannot see those who have
gone before – you are still earthly; they
are heavenly. But you can feel the cloud
of witnesses surrounding you, and you
can have community with those who
are in heaven.

IT IS SIMPLY our human lot to know affliction and endure fear. Let suffering and illness, let temptation and persecution come! These are small things in comparison with the great love God has for us. And the more highly we praise his love, the more powerfully will he stand by us. Indeed, we can defy the whole world, for we are secure in the knowledge that Christ is the Lord; that he can redeem every evil; that in him all powers and principalities must bow down before God.

THOUGH the Holy Spirit itself cannot be explained, its workings can. They demonstrate God's reality. Once this reality touches us, we perceive God; we sense that God is there. If only we were constantly aware of this reality! For truly, it is our duty to walk in the Spirit once we have experienced it, and to carry the reality of God into the most mundane aspects of life. It is our duty to gather everything into the light-circle of the reality of God.

LORD GOD, we praise you for opening your world to us, and for granting us access to the kingdom of heaven through Jesus, your son. We ask you: give us discernment to know the difference between the temporal and the eternal, and clear eyes to see the glory of eternity, also in creation, so that we may be grateful for everything that comes from your hand. Amen.